WHAT YOU SHOULD KNOW ABOUT

A PARENT

WHO DRINKS

TOO MUCH

WHAT YOU SHOULD KNOW ABOUT

A PARENT

WHO DRINKS

TOO MUCH

WILLIAM L. COLEMAN

MINNEAPOLIS

WHAT YOU SHOULD KNOW ABOUT A PARENT WHO DRINKS
TOO MUCH

Cover design: Bob Fuller
Interior design: Jim Brisson

Library of Congress Cataloging-in-Publication Data

Coleman, William L.
    What you should know about a parent who drinks too much
/ William L. Coleman.
        p.   cm.
    Summary: Discusses alcoholism and the problems caused
by a parent who drinks too much and suggests positive, Christian ways of dealing with these difficulties and hurts.
    ISBN 0-8066-2610-0
    1. Children of alcoholics—Juvenile literature. 2. Alcohol-
ism—Juvenile literature. 3. Alcoholism—Religious aspects—
Christianity—Juvenile literature. [1. Alcoholism. 2. Parent and
child. 3. Christian life.] I. Title.
HV5132.C64   1992
362.29'23—dc20   92-18314
                                                          CIP
                                                           AC

The paper used in this publication meets the minimum require-
ments of American National Standard for Information Sciences—
Permanence of Paper for Printed Library Materials, ANSI
Z329.48-1984.   ∞™

Manufactured in the U.S.A.   AF 9-2610

96   95   94   93   92   1   2   3   4   5   6   7   8   9   10

◆ ◆ ◆ ◆ ◆

CONTENTS

CONTENTS

CONTENTS

◆ ◆ ◆ ◆ ◆

ACKNOWLEDGMENTS

In writing this book, not only did I draw on my experience as a child, but I also talked to many people who were willing to share their feelings and knowledge. Some of the kindest people I have met are those who have been the victims of alcohol.

Particularly I want to thank Virginia Nuss, Senior Professional, at North Central Court Referral and Outpatient Counseling Service. Virginia assembled a group of volunteers who gave of themselves in the interest of helping children. They were extremely caring.

Another excellent source was Mike. The child of alcoholic parents and an alcoholic himself, Mike was generous with his time.

I want to thank Liz, Chad, and Connie for reading the material and making good suggestions for improvements.

To protect the identities of those who shared with me, I have not used any of the actual stories I heard.

♦ ♦ ♦ ♦ ♦

Suggestions for Adults

There is a child somewhere who needs help, and you may be exactly the one to help. That child is a victim of a miserable adult problem which he or she barely understands and with which he or she is poorly equipped to cope. An adult has brought pain into the child's life; hopefully other adults, such as yourself, can bring a sense of peace, security, reassurance, and love.

This is no light task; when you reach out to strengthen a young person, you do the work of God. There may be no more rewarding work on earth than to mend a child's broken heart.

There are at least two ways to use this book. One is to give the book to the young person. As a motivated reader, the child can travel through its pages at his or her own speed or pick out chapters that are particularly relevant at the moment. Another approach is for you to read the book with the child or children you have in mind. The human contact and the opportunity to interact is extremely beneficial. Counselors, teachers, parents, and friends make excellent resource people with this book as an effective tool.

As you use the book, keep these guidelines in mind:

    1. *Always tell the truth.* The last thing the child needs is another person to lie to

him or her. He already sees life as quicksand: shifting, deceitful, wearisome, and untrustworthy. Be a straight shooter in that child's world. Honesty is not to be confused with frankness or brashness. The child may not need to be told everything, but what the child is told must be true. Never attempt to couch the facts in lies.

2. *Neither condemn nor defend the drinking parent.* Stick with the facts. The child knows the wrongs of alcoholism. He or she sees it and feels its presence. It simply isn't helpful to depict the parent as immoral or to conjure up pity for the parent. Resist that temptation and deal with the situation at hand.

3. *Set up a regular time to meet with the child.* The young person lacks structure and needs an adult to trust. If you say you can meet together on Thursday at 7:00 P.M., do not break that appointment. Allow plenty of time, and don't hurry. Get together three or four times or whatever you feel is appropriate. The child could use some evidence of stability and caring.

4. *Pace yourself.* Don't push. What the child is not open to discuss today, he or she may be eager to discuss on another occasion. Rapport usually doesn't happen instantly.

5. *Be open to questions.* It is important to get the young person talking. You don't have to be the answer person. If you don't know, say so. The child needs a place to voice his or her fears, doubts, bewilderment, or whatever. When appropriate, use the table of contents and turn to the section that deals with the question being raised.

Bring up questions concerning areas about which you think the child may be wondering. Don't push at some area if you note resistance, but keep in mind that the young person might not always know what questions to ask.

The time you spend together lets the child know that he or she matters to both you and God. Even short sessions of love, attention, and help can make a tremendous difference in the young person's life.

◆ ◆ ◆ ◆ ◆

It's a Great Life!

Have you ever seen a circus performer or a squirrel walk across a high wire? Have you ridden on a water slide or raced down the sidewalk on a skateboard? We have all kinds of fantastic things to do and places to go.

But even a great life can have some hard knocks and big disappointments. This book is written with the hope that, even when things get tough, you will be able to see a bright and shiny tomorrow.

May God walk by your side every day, and may the two of you become the best of friends.

Bill Coleman

◆ ◆ ◆ ◆ ◆

What Is an Alcoholic?

Suppose there was a person who shoplifted a penknife and was caught by the police. After he was released, the person went back and shoplifted a second knife and was caught a second time. The person is getting into big trouble, but he steals a third one, and a fourth.

The knives aren't worth it. The person gets into trouble and his family becomes embarrassed and angry. The shoplifter goes to jail for a week and pays a large fine.

But what if after all of that misery and trouble, the person goes back and steals a fifth penknife? By then you know beyond any doubt that this person has a serious problem.

Alcoholics do something similar. They continue to drink alcohol even though the drinking hurts them and the people around them.

The alcohol hurts their health, affects their job, slows their mind, injures their marriage, frightens their children, causes financial problems, gets them into arguments and fights, and creates trouble with the police.

When alcohol makes a person do some or all of these things and the person still drinks alcohol, that person is probably an alcoholic. Many people drink alcohol and never create a problem. But those who repeatedly cause trouble from drinking are most likely alcoholics.

Don't expect the alcoholic to believe this. Almost always he or she will insist that alcohol is no problem. The alcoholic will assure you that he or she can control the drinking at any time. But the alcoholic continues to drink and create problems because of his or her drinking.

Drinking alcohol has always been a risky business. Too much can change one's personality, behavior, and ability to think. Alcoholics suffer from all of these because they can't control their drinking.

"Wine is a mocker and beer a brawler; whoever is led astray by them is not wise" (Proverbs 20:1).

♦ ♦ ♦ ♦ ♦

What Is Alcohol?

Exactly what is alcohol? Alcohol is a colorless liquid with the chemical name of C_2H_6O. It is usually found in fermented or distilled liquor such as beer, wine, or whiskey. Alcohol has the ability to intoxicate the drinker. To be intoxicated means that the drinker's physical and mental abilities are changed for at least a while.

When someone drinks a beverage with alcohol in it, that person will be affected one way while a friend may be affected another way. How much alcohol is in the drink, how much the person drinks, how often he or she drinks, his or her size, and how much the person has had to eat all affect whether or not he or she gets drunk. No two people are exactly the same. Some people may get drunk faster than others because of the way their bodies are made up.

Usually a drink of whiskey has a higher alcohol content than wine has, and wine has more alcohol than beer, but the amount a person drinks determines how soon he or she will become drunk. Nine cans of beer can be just as intoxicating as half a bottle of whiskey.

A person may say, "I'm not much of a drinker; I just drink a dozen beers or so on Saturday nights while I watch the ball game." But that's the same as drinking two-thirds of a bottle of

17

whiskey. Yet, he or she thinks it is safe because it is "only" beer.

Another person may say, "I only drink a little wine with my meals. Last night I drank a bottle of wine." That person drank the same as a third of a bottle of whiskey. The person thinks he or she didn't have much alcohol, but that is not the case. The good news is that the person ate a meal with the drink and that probably helped him or her become less intoxicated.

Not everyone who drinks whiskey, wine, or beer gets drunk. Millions drink in moderation and *never* become drunk. They control how much alcohol comes into their bodies, and alcohol doesn't become a problem. Not everyone who drinks alcohol is an alcoholic. But some people apparently can't control how much they drink after the first few. Neither can they control what it does to their bodies. For them, drinking alcoholic beverages becomes an extremely serious problem.

◆ ◆ ◆ ◆ ◆

How Do I Know My Parent Has a Drinking Problem?

Family members will probably know there is a drinking problem before the drinker knows it. The person who drinks too much is busy denying that there is a problem. The person who drinks thinks his or her drinking is normal or that it is necessary or that it is fun.

The best proof that your parent has a drinking problem is a big change in your parent's behavior. Many adults will have a drink of alcohol or two and become a "little" high. They might talk more, act a bit silly, or possibly even become quiet.

But the problem drinker changes drastically. Alcohol seems to make the person:

act mean

have slurred speech

become forgetful

get too loud

lose body control

lose his or her balance

become terribly rude

hurt people

say cruel things

repeatedly get sick

have big mood changes.

Possibly your parent has had a drinking problem all of your life and you don't notice much change. But if your parent drinks alcohol and acts in the ways described, he or she almost certainly has a drinking problem.

Another way to check for a drinking problem is to look at your parent's drinking habits. The following might suggest a problem:

a sharp increase in your parent's drinking

a need to always have alcohol in his or her hand

drinking in the morning to "get started"

"binge drinking" (not necessarily drinking often but getting drunk when he or she does drink)

the need for alcohol to "calm me down."

These are only a few of the possible changes. Children aren't doctors or counselors or social workers. You can't tell for certain whether your parent has a problem. But if you see some of these signs, go to someone you can trust and tell that person what is going on. He or she might be able to help.

Some good people to talk to are teachers, counselors, pastors, grandparents, your other parent, or older brothers or sisters. Don't simply sit and worry. Find someone with whom to share your concern.

If you think you see signs of your parent having a drinking problem, *tell someone.*

Words We Use

When alcoholism or drinking problems are discussed, often unusual words and phrases are used. You may not understand them, and so you simply guess what they mean. To help you understand, here are some terms and their definitions:

Addiction—A harmful habit that we are unable to stop or control on our own. Food, drugs, and alcohol can all be addictive.

Alcoholics Anonymous (AA)—An organization that helps people to stop drinking and remain sober. They hold small-group meetings. Those who attend receive information and encouragement. There are also groups for spouses, families, and young people.

Codependent—A person whose life and behavior are changed because someone else has a drinking problem.

Cravings—A deep physical desire for more alcohol. That need for a drink has control of a person's behavior.

D.T.'s (delirium tremens)—Daydreams or nightmares while the person is still awake. An alcoholic may have these when he or she first stops drinking.

Detoxification—The process of alcohol emptying from a person's system when he or she stops drinking. Detox centers are available to help people go through this difficult process.

D.W.I. or D.U.I.—If a person is arrested for driving while there is too much alcohol in his or her blood, he or she can be charged with Driving While Intoxicated or Driving Under the Influence. Some states have severe penalties for these offenses. The driver could lose his or her license, receive a fine, go to jail, or be placed on probation.

On the wagon—The person has stopped drinking.

Sobriety test—The police may make a person take a test to see whether he or she has been drinking too much or if there is too much alcohol in his or her blood.

Treatment center—A place where people can find help to stop drinking.

Withdrawal symptoms—When an alcoholic goes without alcohol for a period of time, he or she could feel sick, get dizzy, have chills or sweat, get severe headaches, and be unable to think well.

The Alcohol Elevator

David said, "I like to drink alcohol because it helps perk me up. I feel more alert and I have more fun."

But Sarah said, "I drink alcohol when I am nervous or excited. A good drink helps calm me down, and then I'm ready for almost anything."

Can a glass of the same stuff perk one person up and calm another person down? Both David and Sarah are right. It all depends on the person and how much alcohol he or she drinks. Remember that no two people are exactly the same. We can only explain what usually happens. You might know someone who reacts in a totally opposite way.

A little bit of alcohol will perk up or stimulate the brain. The drinker seems to become brightcr, more talkative, a bit bolder, maybe more fun to be with. The elevator is going up, and the trip is pleasant.

However, with a few too many drinks, the elevator makes a sudden stop and then starts going down. The alcohol is now working to depress the brain of the drinker. Speech may become slurred, and actions become slow and clumsy. The drinker's personality may become a little duller.

While the elevator is going up and down, the drinker may have all kinds of moods. He or she may brag, joke around, talk loud, get angry, be demanding, insult everyone, start arguments and fights, cry, laugh, pout, pass out, fall down, sing, give money away, yell, flatter, flirt, do or say practically anything. *The person loses control* as alcohol takes over.

If a person uses alcohol to change his or her mood—to perk up or slow down—the person is taking a risk. Will he or she use the correct amount, or will the person forget and drink too much? Will he or she try to solve a serious problem by simply drinking too much? Alcohol can be especially dangerous if we use it to change our personality and allow it to influence our daily lives.

What Is It Like to Be Drunk?

Did you ever go on rides at an amusement park? Have you ridden a roller coaster or gone on a ride that rapidly twirls around in circles? When some people get off those rides, they feel dizzy, their legs are wobbly, and they have trouble talking or seeing. That sensation is close to what it physically feels like to be drunk.

Fortunately that feeling lasts for only a few minutes after a person gets off a ride at the park. But people who drink too much alcohol stay that way, sometimes for hours.

Imagine trying to drive a car or trying to work or trying to get along with your family when you are dizzy, have trouble standing, and can't see well.

When people are drunk they can't think correctly. Often they have trouble remembering what they said or promised. People who are drunk may get loud or terribly quiet. They may say things that they don't mean. Drunk people may be rough and hurt people who get close to them.

People who are drunk are out of control. Any number of bad things can happen when people can't control themselves. When drunk people get sober they often have trouble remembering exactly what they did while they were drunk.

Drunkenness is extremely dangerous. It isn't just a harmless, playful activity that adults like to do. Drunk people fall down, have accidents, get into fights, say terrible things, and frequently hurt the people they love.

Some people spend too much money when they are drunk, and their families suffer because the parents can't pay the bills.

Because drunk people lose control and can hurt people, the Bible teaches us to not get drunk. The God who gave us the Bible wants us to be happy and safe. Drunkenness endangers our happiness and the happiness of others.

"Do not get drunk on wine" (Ephesians 5:18a).

◆ ◆ ◆ ◆ ◆

Why Do They Drink Too Much?

Why do some people drink alcohol until they can't think straight? Why do they drink until they can't talk or stand well or drive a car correctly? Why do they keep drinking until they say mean things, hurt people's feelings, and the next day can't remember what they did?

26

Those are tough questions to answer. The best we can do is to tell you where to find the answer. It is in one of these three boxes.

Box 1 Body Chemistry	**Box 2** Personal Choices	**Box 3** Chemistry and Choices

Box 1: Some doctors think that people who drink to get drunk and do it often can't help themselves. Some doctors believe that a glass of alcohol makes certain people's bodies crave more alcohol, and they cannot stop drinking. If that is the case, these people should never use alcohol.

Box 2: Others believe that drinking to the point of being drunk is always a personal choice. If we refuse to say no, it is our own fault if we become intoxicated. All people need to make decisions and control themselves.

Box 3: Maybe the answer is a little bit of both. Some people may not handle alcohol well, and they become drunk easily. But all drinking is an individual decision, and everyone needs to know how to say no.

Whatever the exact answer may be, this we do know: None of us should do anything to hurt ourselves or anyone else.

Evcryone needs to control him- or herself.

Whether a person has a chemical problem or is simply making bad choices, he must be willing to take responsibility for his own behavior. Eventually he has to accept help for his problem. No one else can make his decision for him.

"Do not join those who drink too much wine" (Proverbs 23:20).

What Is a Hangover?

When we over-do something, our bodies react. If we exercise too much, our bodies cry out in pain. If we eat too much, our stomachs become uncomfortable and we become sluggish. When we go too long without sleep, our bodies slow down and don't work as well.

Our bodies and minds need balance. If we have too much or too little of something, our bodies complain about being mistreated.

A person who drinks too much overloads the body's systems with alcohol. His or her body shouts out in protest and tries to throw off the extra beer or wine or whiskey. A hangover is the body's attempt to protect itself from abuse.

The morning after a person has had too much to drink, he or she may wake up as the body is trying to correct itself. That person will probably have a throbbing headache, feel terribly sick, throw up (maybe often), possibly have shaking hands, make frequent trips to the bathroom, and have trouble standing or walking.

Hangovers are so miserable that the drinker may promise him- or herself to never drink that much again. Why would anyone knowingly go through this kind of agony?

Unfortunately, the person soon forgets the pain and discomfort. Too soon the person again drinks too much alcohol and has another terrible hangover.

Hangovers look funny in the movies. We laugh when we see someone look so miserable. An actor holds his head and stumbles around and groans and makes hilarious faces. Some people think it is humorous to watch another person temporarily out of control.

But it isn't so funny when the person with the hangover is a parent. Mothers and fathers with hangovers are sick at the time, and that sickness can be harmful to the people they care about the most.

◆ ◆ ◆ ◆ ◆

Do They Drink Because of Me?

Sometimes, all alone and feeling down, you start to think strange thoughts. You wonder if maybe, just possibly, it could be true that your parent drinks too much because of you.

Many children of drinking parents ask that question. It is as if the drinking problem were a huge puzzle with one large piece still missing, and they wonder, "Am I the missing piece of the puzzle? Maybe I am the piece that goes in the middle."

But why would parents drink because of a child?

Do they drink because you were born?

Do they drink because you are disobedient?

Do they drink because you are noisy?

Do they drink because you are a girl or a boy?

Do they drink because you are expensive?

Do they drink because you complain?

Do they drink because you are messy?

The answer to all these questions is no.

People don't drink too much because of other people. Even if they say they drink because of the children, it isn't true. They may think it is true, but it isn't. The reason people drink is inside them. The missing piece of the puzzle is somewhere in your parent. It is *never* in you.

A Lot of Families Like Yours

A girl sat in a classroom and thought there was no one else who had her problems. Her mother was an alcoholic, and life was often hard at home. She never knew when her mother would be drinking too much. Family members screamed at each other. The girl felt nervous and uneasy much of the time.

Sitting in a room with twenty-five other children, the girl wondered if anyone had ever felt the way she felt. The girl believed she was different and must be a weird person.

It is terrible to feel alone. It is awful to think that there is something wrong with you. No one likes to be different if he or she thinks the difference is bad.

31

If this girl could talk to all the other children in the room, she would probably find that there are five, six, or seven other students who have parents who drink too much. She is far from being alone.

The girl would have to talk to the other students because she couldn't tell whether their parents were alcoholic by looking at them. They don't wear badges that say, "My parents drink too much." They don't all wear their hair a certain way or wear the same kind of shoes.

The best-dressed person in the room could have parents who drink too much. So could the child in shabby clothes as could the smartest student, the slowest student, the funniest student, or the quiet one who sits alone. Children of alcoholics are all around us, and they know what this girl is going through because they see, hear, and feel the same things.

Sometimes we think people can tell by looking at us that our families have a drinking problem. That isn't true. Rich families, poor families, traveling families, athletic families, religious families, motorcycle-riding families can all have members who drink too much.

It isn't easy to live with someone who drinks too much. We can ask God to help us not think that we are alone and weird. Some of the children you enjoy being around the most might have an alcohol problem at their house, too.

◆ ◆ ◆ ◆ ◆

People Who Forgive
Are Happier

When the school bell finally rang, Linda was out of her chair, darting for the door. All week long she had thought about Friday night. Right after dinner, Linda would grab some chips and half a dozen tapes and head for Felicia's house.

Five or six of Linda's friends would be there. They would play games, listen to music, and laugh late into the night. Thinking about it had made Linda's entire week go better.

Bouncing into the house, Linda soon saw her dreams for the evening come unglued. Her mother had come home from work early and had already had several drinks just to "relax." The alcohol was affecting her mood and messing with her mind.

Soon Linda and her mother were talking in heated tones. Her mother couldn't remember saying that Linda could go out tonight, so she would have to stay home. Besides, her mother insisted, she might need Linda to run errands.

Linda went to her room and cried. She didn't come out to eat, and her mother grew angrier. Linda felt betrayed, belittled, humiliated, and cheated. For days she didn't talk to her mother.

When something like this happens, it cuts right through to your heart. This is no way to treat anyone. It's a dirty deal. And what hurts even more is that it could happen again.

While we might have trouble forgiving and forgetting, what choice do we have? If we think about an unfair situation every day, we will become bitter and maybe even mean. If we try to get even, we make a bad situation worse.

The best thing we can do for ourselves is to forgive our drinking parent. That is not easy. Sometimes we are unable to forgive unless God gives us the power to do so. We need to ask God to help us. Forgiving our parent is best for us and best for him or her. When bad things happen that aren't our fault, forgiving whomever caused the trouble will take some of the pain away so that we can start living a less stressful life.

"Bear with each other and forgive whatever grievances you may have against one another. Forgive as the Lord forgave you" (Colossians 3:13).

◆ ◆ ◆ ◆ ◆

God Isn't Upset
with You

Once in a while Matt's parents would get loud and scream at each other late at night. The noise and threats scared Matt, and he would pull the covers up over his head. Alone and frightened, Matt often wondered if he had done something terrible and God was punishing his family.

No one in Matt's house seemed very happy. Some days they would go along all right, but on most days a fight would start.

Matt began to look at the way he lived. Maybe God was angry because he cussed sometimes, he thought. Or perhaps God was upset about Matt not getting his homework done. If he decided to do his homework, possibly then God would quiet his family down. More than once his eyes filled with tears as he tried to figure out what he was doing wrong.

God doesn't act like that. God doesn't make families miserable because a boy leaves his bed unmade. God doesn't watch a girl cross the street on a don't-walk signal and decide to make the windows in her house crack just to teach her a lesson. God spends his time looking for ways to help families.

It is God's intention that families should live in peace, love, and friendship. That's why God created them. And God is there to help families do that, because they really can't live harmonious lives on their own.

The next time there is trouble at your house, tell yourself that it isn't your fault and it isn't God's fault. God loved you enough to send his only Son to die for your sins. God is not in the business of knocking children around. God is in the business of helping—so ask for a little help.

The Bible tells us that Jesus promises to travel through life with us. He is a friend.

Jesus said, "I have called you friends" (John 15:15b).

◆ ◆ ◆ ◆ ◆

Be Happy to Be Happy

When things are going tough, some people sit down and pout about the hard times. They feel sad and wish life could go a little better. Most of us have days—or even weeks or months—of feeling sorry for ourselves.

If we pout for too long, we might forget how to be happy. Can you imagine someone forgetting how to laugh? Try to picture someone teaching his face how to smile: "Now let's get with it, face. Pull those cheeks back. Spread those lips. Make those eyes sparkle. Come on now, open those eyelids."

It would be miserable to live in a world where people forgot how to smile. Everyone would look like a tired bulldog.

When you have the chance to be happy, you need to go ahead and take it. There will be plenty of times to mope and worry and grump. Call a friend and see if he or she can play ball today. Ask someone to go down to the lake with you and skip stones across the water.

Too many children are afraid to be happy. They think that if they become happy they will only be hurt later. They don't trust happiness. Happiness is a friend. Our friend can't stay around all of the time, but happiness is a great deal of fun when we let it stick close.

This is a great day to be happy. Who wants to feel down all the time? Think of something you could enjoy, and go for the goodness.

"Be happy, young man, while you are young,
And let your heart give you joy in the days of your youth" (Ecclesiastes 11:9a).

◆ ◆ ◆ ◆ ◆

Parents Can Say Dumb Things

All of us say stupid things sometimes. We don't mean our words to come out as harshly as they sound. Later we wish we could take the words back, chop them up, and burn them.

But words aren't made of wood. Neither are they paper that we can crumple into a ball and toss in the wastebasket. Words have a way of hurting, and sometimes the pain stays around for a long time.

When people drink too much, they don't think very well. Sometimes they say dumb things that they probably wouldn't say if they weren't using alcohol.

A parent might say, "That dress looks terrible. Take it off." That would be a cruel thing to say, and it would hurt. If the person had not been drinking, he or she would probably never say something mean. Later, when the effects of alcohol have worn off, the daughter might find out that her parent likes the dress.

She shouldn't throw the dress away or hang it up and never wear it again. Sometime when her parent has not been drinking, she might ask, "Do you think I should wear the blue dress tonight?" Maybe she will find out that her parent really *doesn't* like the dress. But she should be sure to ask again.

When parents are drinking, they might say dumb things like: "You are grounded for a month" or "Take those books out and burn them" or "I don't want you playing with her."

Keep your cool. When your parent is not drinking, politely give it another try.

"Reckless words pierce like a sword" (Proverbs 12:18a).

◆ ◆ ◆ ◆ ◆

Feeling Angry

Some days you want to slam doors, shout, and throw a shoe at your dog. You get fed up with the mess. Why should you have to put up with a parent who drinks too much? Did you ever want to hit something—a wall, a cupboard, or a person? When you are angry you feel like you have had it, and if something doesn't change, you are going to blow up.

Have you ever felt pressure building up inside your body and inside your brain? Have you ever felt so angry that you thought you were going to lose control of yourself? Have you ever cried because you felt frustrated? Did you want to cry so badly that it took all your strength to hold it in? Sometimes children are afraid to show their anger or to feel angry because their parents might punish them.

The children of parents who drink too much often get angry. That's easy to understand. When many things go wrong and we can't do anything to change them, anger is the natural reaction. Anger is normal. But too much anger, too often, can cause you to do some ridiculous things that you could soon regret. Here are a few guidelines to help keep your emotions from getting out of hand.

1. *Anger is normal.* You aren't an evil or mean person because you get angry.

2. *Anger can hurt you.* That nervous, raging feeling inside can do damage to your body and mind.

3. *Anger can hurt others.* If you go too far with anger, you could hurt someone else, maybe even your dog.

4. *Anger should be spoken.* Who can you tell about your anger—a parent, friend, brother, sister, teacher, or God? Talking about it helps control it.

5. *Anger affects your thinking.* It is hard to think correctly when we are angry, so we are likely to do dumb things.

6. *Anger needs to be short.* Be angry, say something about it, and get over it. If you

stay angry for a long time, you begin to cause trouble for yourself. Anger over a long period of time turns into bitterness and makes you miserable.

7. *Four steps for dealing with anger:*

   a. Identify exactly what you are angry about. Don't be angry at everything. Draw a bull's-eye and say those are the things that make your blood boil.

   b. Talk. When possible go to the person who made you angry. If you can't go to that person, talk to someone else. Don't bottle up your anger.

   c. Accept the fact that there will be things you can't change.

   d. Forgive people every time you can.

8. *Anger comes from fear.* If you are afraid of what might happen next, you are likely to stay angry. Tell an adult what you are afraid of. The adult might be able to explain what is going on, change the situation, or help protect you.

Anger can be useful if it isn't allowed to run wild.

" 'In your anger do not sin': Do not let the sun go down while you are still angry" (Ephesians 4:26).

41

◆ ◆ ◆ ◆ ◆

Someone to Talk To

When Ted got his new baseball glove, he carried it everywhere. He put it in his desk at school and took it to the lunchroom. Rain stopped him from playing outside at recess, so Ted stood in the hall pounding a ball into his glove.

After school the clouds cleared out as Ted walked home. As he came close to Captain Benson's house, he could see the retired sea captain sitting on his porch. Quickening his step, Ted hurried down the street to Captain Benson's place.

Captain Benson looked the glove over and read the name inside. It was a Dale Murphy glove. He pulled at the leather straps and told Ted what a good-looking piece of equipment it was. Naturally Captain Benson began pounding the baseball into the pocket. No one can resist doing that to a glove.

Everybody needs someone to talk to, a special somebody who will listen to how you feel, a person who treats you like you are important.

It is even better if you have more than one person to talk to. Friends can be good listeners. So can school teachers or counselors. Parents, brothers, sisters, grandparents, aunts, and uncles often understand how you feel. Pastors are usually patient and kind.

When something good happens, we want to share the news. We like to see our friend smile and be glad with us. In the same way, it is important to talk to another person when something bad comes into our lives. Many times we simply need to say it out loud. At other times we need someone's opinion or advice about what we should do.

Talking to mirrors can be fun. We can even make a few faces and laugh at ourselves. Writing in diaries is private and mysterious. Sharing with a gray-brown spotted cat or a lazy long-eared dog might help. But talking to a special person is hard to beat. People know how to understand—when we feel great and when we feel lousy.

◆ ◆ ◆ ◆ ◆

Why Doesn't God Stop Her?

When Derrick was little, his Aunt Pat told him that he should pray every day. She told him to tell God what he wanted, and God would answer his prayers.

Derrick believed his aunt, so he told God that he wanted a bike and a computer and a video game and expensive basketball shoes. He received the shoes for his birthday, and the bike arrived at Christmas. Derrick never did get the computer or the video game. But he was happy: two out of four wasn't bad. When he needed or wanted something, Derrick made it a point to talk to God. He prayed a lot just before his birthday and Christmas.

A couple of years later Derrick's mother began drinking too much alcohol, and that presented some serious problems. After a few months of trouble, the boy started talking to God, and he asked God to take the desire for alcohol away from his mother.

Derrick prayed often and hard, but his mother drank just as much as ever. Finally he stopped talking to God. He was angry that God didn't answer his prayers.

Did God ignore Derrick? Was God mad at Derrick? Was God too weak to help Derrick?

None of those reasons seem correct. Maybe the real reason is that God doesn't change people who aren't ready to change. God doesn't usually rush in and take the gun out of a robber's hands. And if a man jumps off the garage roof, God probably isn't going to catch him. But if people want God to help them change, God will change them.

God cares about Derrick's mother and the problem they share. I wouldn't be surprised if God even cries for Derrick's mother. But God is leading her to the point where *she* wants to change.

Derrick should continue to talk to God. He might ask God to help his mother see the need to change. He might ask God to bring people into her life whom she could trust to help. God loves Derrick and his mother and wants to help her change.

"I urge, then, first of all, that requests, prayers, intercession and thanksgiving be made for everyone" (1 Timothy 2:1).

Blamed for Crazy Things

Have you ever been blamed for leaving the door open when you knew you didn't do it? Did you ever get yelled at for leaving the milk on the table when you never used the milk?

None of us likes to get blamed for things we didn't do. It hurts to be accused of something when you know you are completely innocent. But it happens. Children, adults, grandparents, dogs, cats, governors, and even the stars get blamed for things they didn't do. A man had a car accident and said that it happened because the stars were in an unusual place that day. The poor stars get accused of the craziest things!

Some of us have learned to handle blame fairly well. We still don't like it, but we know that being blamed happens. We don't let it worry us for very long. Many times children are better at shaking it off than adults are.

A parent is wrong for blaming a child for something the child didn't do. And wrong is never the right thing for a parent to do. But the child needs to understand what is going on. The parent is saying something ridiculous because the parent is not in control. The parent is drinking too much.

When your parent drinks too much, he or she might accuse you of some crazy things, some silly things, some absolutely ridiculous things. But you need to remember: that's the alcohol talking. When people drink too much, they can't think straight, they can't remember correctly, and often they exaggerate in what they say.

It is important to understand what is happening. Understanding doesn't make your parent behave better, but at least you know what really is going on. How do you get understanding? God working through others can help. Talk to someone you can trust about your problem.

◆ ◆ ◆ ◆ ◆

Play Line Ball

Call a couple of friends and ask them to play line ball with you. It's easy to learn. You don't need many players. You don't need a large field. And everyone gets to bat.

Don't spend too much time sitting at home worrying about your parent's drinking problem.

The game is simple. One or more people bat. One person pitches, and one or more people play in the field. And no one has to run bases. The game can be played with only a few people. It is fast moving and provides good exercise, and you don't have to be a great athlete to play. Both boys and girls can play line ball. There are no teams. Everyone gets to win some and lose some.

Don't spend too much time sitting at home worrying about your parent's drinking problem.

Suppose you are the batter. You are allowed three swings of the bat. How do you get a hit?

1. If the ball goes past the pitcher in the air, it is a single.

2. If the ball goes over the pitcher's head, it is a double.

3. If the ball goes over the fielder's head, it is a home run.

There are no bases.

There are three ways to get out:

1. You miss the ball on three swings.

2. You hit a ball and it bounces in front of the pitcher.

3. Someone catches the ball in the air.

After three outs, your team goes into the field and the other team comes up to bat.

Don't spend too much time sitting at home worrying about your parent's drinking problem.

Everyone remembers who is on what base and how many runs have been scored. They also keep track of how many outs there are. If you want, change the rules to fit your own game. Have fun and get a few good hits.

Don't spend too much time sitting at home worrying about your parent's drinking problem.

◆ ◆ ◆ ◆ ◆

Can You Change Your Parents?

Do you ever wish there was a button to push or a handle or a key to turn that would make everything different? Do you ever wonder if there is a word or a sentence or a promise you could say that would make the problem disappear? Have you ever wanted to go down to the drugstore and buy a bottle of medicine that would cure your parent of the alcohol problem?

If you have done any of these, you are like millions of other children. They wish they could do something to change their parent's behavior.

Some children try to hide the alcohol so their parents can't find it. That usually makes the parents angry or confused, and they only buy more alcohol.

Other children might pretend they are sick and hope their parents will feel sorry for them. Most of the time these children simply miss school and get behind in their work.

Still others clean up their rooms and try to be extra neat. They wonder if their parents drink too much because they are unhappy with them. It is always good to have a clean room, but people don't abuse alcohol because of unmade beds or towels on the floor.

We hear of children who get angry and speak harshly to their parents and tell them they had better stop drinking. Parents need to know they are hurting their children, but "chewing them out" doesn't usually help, and sometimes the parents not only yell back but also hurt the children.

All of us would like to change the person with the drinking problem, but we cannot change other people. People who drink too much must want to stop drinking. If they want to stop, counselors, support groups, or even friends might help.

But if a parent doesn't want to change, a child cannot change him or her. It isn't your fault if your parent drinks too much, and you cannot make him or her stop.

◆ ◆ ◆ ◆ ◆

Videos in Your Mind

How many good times can you remember having with your parents? There may have been bad times, too, but what about the good times?

Do you ever bake cookies, make popcorn, or laugh while you make funny faces? Do you ever play with a cat or dog on the floor and feel great about being with your mother or father? Some of us have trouble remembering the good times, but others of us can picture them in our memories. Like running a video through our minds, we can see our families singing together or playing ball or running through a sprinkler on the lawn.

Some children don't have any good mind-videos about their parents. They have tried to remember some good times but can't find them in their memories.

Other children have good mind-videos, but they seldom play them. Each time they think of their parents they begin running the bad or unpleasant mind-videos over and over again.

50

The problem with playing the bad videos all the time is that we forget the good ones. Before long we might not want to play the mind-videos about our parents at all.

I can picture my father walking across a large park with me running alongside him. We stopped and sat on a bench for a while and talked. Then he walked some more and I ran and climbed a tree and then hurried back to him.

Later in the day we stopped at a small restaurant and ordered cheese omelets. It felt great to sit next to my dad and be close to him.

Not every mind-video about my dad is a good one. But when I remember the happy times and see them in my memory, it makes me feel good all over.

Do you have any favorite mind-videos about your parents? Play the ones that are fun.

"Finally, brothers, whatever is true, whatever is noble, whatever is right, whatever is pure, whatever is lovely, whatever is admirable—if anything is excellent or praiseworthy—think about such things" (Philippians 4:8).

◆ ◆ ◆ ◆ ◆

Some Tough Thoughts

When we feel a great deal of pressure and hurt inside, many of us think some terrible things. We want the pain to go away, even if it means that someone else has to get hurt. You may think some tough thoughts. All of us do sometimes. For instance, you may have thought, *I hate my drinking parent.*

A lot of children in alcoholic families feel that way. They hate the alcohol and what it does to their family, and they think they hate their parents, too.

Hate is a strong feeling. It would be better for everyone if you could separate the problem from your parent. You can hate a situation and wish it were better. Some children have not been able to stop hating. That is understandable. However, the day may come when you can drop the hate.

Some children might think, *I wish my parent would get into a bad car accident.* They want something to happen that will stop their parent from drinking. So far nothing has worked. The yelling, the anger, the disappointment, the confusion, and the alcohol go on. Desperate, they wish for something that will end the problem once and for all. Maybe a serious accident would make the parent realize how bad things are. Some children wish the accident would end their parent's life.

Those are tough thoughts, but they aren't uncommon. The person who thinks them isn't weird or mean or evil. He or she just wants a solution and can't think of anything else that will help.

Have you ever thought, *I wish my parent would get a terrible disease?* Sometimes children wish that because they love their parent so much. They think that if the parent were restricted to a bed or a wheelchair, maybe the parent would leave alcohol alone.

Don't feel guilty about what you think. When we live in a bad situation we might imagine anything. If we try to love someone who hurts us in return, our minds become extremely confused.

But never act on an unhealthy thought. Let it pass out of your mind just the way it came in. And pray that a real, lasting solution can be found for your parent's problem.

◆ ◆ ◆ ◆ ◆

The Yelling Scares Me

At a ball game yelling can make a lot of sense. The players are excited, and they scream at each other to run faster, hit harder, and slide farther. The fans and the cheerleaders also holler at the top of their lungs. It is all right to be noisy at the right time and in the right place.

It is often good to yell when someone is in trouble or danger. When a person is about to step in front of a moving train, a loud scream could save his life. Or if you see someone about to walk off a roof, you would be right to yell. If a kid were going to dive into an empty swimming pool, it would be a good time to shout something. That's what God made yelling for.

Yelling has its place, and screaming at people in anger isn't it—especially if a parent or another adult is screaming at a child. Screaming at a child is verbal violence. It hurts the child inside just as if he or she were beaten in the heart. Imagine if you could hit someone's soul or pound their spirit.

It is a different story when a child yells at another child. The words might hurt, but they don't bruise the sense of self-worth. That is not to say that it is okay to rag on another kid.

When an adult speaks harshly or even cruelly, however, a child is more likely to believe what the adult says—especially if that adult is a parent.

If a parent says, "You're dumb," "You're stupid," "You're lazy," "You're a pain," or "You're no good," the child may think it is true because his or her own mother or father says it.

What if your parent yells at you when he or she drinks too much? Here are a few helpful suggestions:

1. *Tell yourself it isn't true.* The mean or ugly things being said about you are a result of the alcohol talking. You aren't dumb or stupid or whatever.

2. *Talk to your nondrinking parent about it if at all possible.* If you don't have a nondrinking parent, find someone else to tell.

3. *Don't yell back.* By screaming in return, you simply add to the noise level and risk making the parent angrier.

Yelling is hard to handle. It is *extremely* important to find someone to talk to about your feelings.

◆ ◆ ◆ ◆ ◆

If There's Danger

Let's imagine you were playing in your backyard in Hawaii. Suddenly there was a terrible
volcanic eruption with fire and hot lava shooting
in all directions. The huge eruption started a gi-
gantic mud slide, and the mud began to pour
down the mountain directly toward your backyard.

What do you think you would do? Would
you stand still and dare the mud to come your
way? Would you decide to stay in your yard and
swim in the mud? Would you close your eyes,
put your arms over your head, and hope the mud
wall would stop? Would you get angry at the
mud and make an ugly face at it? Of course not.
You'd get out of your backyard before you got
hurt. And you would tell anyone else to get out
of the yard, too.

What if a child was being hit or physically
abused by a drunken parent? Would you tell the
child to simply stand still and let the parent hit
him or her? Would you tell the child to close his
or her eyes and cover his or her head and hope
the parent goes away? What if the child gets a
cut lip, a black eye, an injured head, or a broken
bone? Would you tell him or her to stay anyway?

Often abused children don't want to leave
the house or tell anyone because they don't want

anyone to know their parents have a drinking problem. Everyone is busy keeping it quiet. But hitting people is dangerous, and it has to be stopped.

Don't even think of running away. The life of a runaway can be just as dangerous.

If the hitting begins, call for help immediately. Don't wait for a broken bone. Go next door to a neighbor. Then call a family member, teacher, pastor, or school counselor. You may have to call 911 for the police.

When a parent who is drinking too much alcohol begins to physically hurt family members, *action must be taken.* Remove yourself at once. Don't stand still and hope the mud slide will go away. You will be helping yourself and your parent.

◆ ◆ ◆ ◆ ◆

What Do Other People Think?

When Troy got a new pair of tennis shoes he put them on and went directly into his backyard. Once there he shuffled his feet in the dirt and tried to get his new white shoes just a little dirty. He had to do it right. Troy wanted his shoes to look good but not too good. He didn't want his friends to tease him or talk about his new shoes. What other people said and thought were very important to Troy.

That's the tricky business of peer pressure. We want other people to notice us but only when we are doing the right things at the right times. We want them to see our new jacket but not the loose thread hanging from the seam.

When someone has a drinking problem, his or her family worries a lot about what other people will think. They work hard to cover up the situation and keep it a secret. Try as much as they can, other people usually get some hint that there is trouble, and some are almost certain to find out about the problem. What are they likely to think? No matter how much we try to cover over our tennis shoes, some people are going to notice. Try to keep these guidelines in mind when worrying about what others think:

1. *Some people are going to find out.* No matter how careful or clever or secretive your family is, the word will leak out. Accept that fact. Others will know that your family is not perfect. But, then, no family is perfect.

2. *Since other people will find out, you might as well share your problem with a trusted friend or counselor.* Trying to hide your situation hurts the people in your family.

Finding someone to talk to could help you.

3. *A few people* won't *understand.* They don't like "drunks," and they stay away from families where there are "drunks." These people don't know what lies behind alcohol abuse. Try to accept people like this, and don't hate them because of their ignorance.

4. *Many people* will *understand.* We are getting better educated about the problems of alcohol. More people realize how much the family members of alcoholics hurt. These people do less judging and more loving. Millions of "other people" have also had family members who have had problems with alcohol. They have had your same experiences, and they do understand.

Don't spend too much time worrying about what other people think. When you find someone who accepts you as the person you are, be his or her friend and keep that friendship close.

◆ ◆ ◆ ◆ ◆

The Fear of Being
Left Alone

What would you do if something happened to both of your parents? What would you do if one of your parents went to the hospital and the other parent started drinking too much? If one or both of your parents have serious problems, you have probably wondered what would become of you. Those aren't strange questions. Many children ask themselves these questions when things seem unstable at home.

If you have those questions, it is important that you ask them. You need to know—like any child—what would happen to you if both of your parents faced a crisis or an emergency. Who can best answer that question for you? Go over this list and see who fits your situation.

1. *Ask your sober parent.* Say something like, "If you are in a car accident and Mom (Dad) is drinking too much or drunk, what should I do? Where should I go?"

2. *Ask a close relative.* If you have only one parent or if both parents have a drinking problem, ask a grandparent, aunt, uncle, or older brother or sister.

3. *Ask a counselor or teacher.* Don't let your questions get you down. If this is something you need to know, go to an adult who works with children and explain your concern.

Every child should have some idea of what will happen in an emergency. If being left alone bothers you, be sure and ask someone about it.

◆ ◆ ◆ ◆ ◆

Feeling Sorry for Yourself

Did you ever want to stay in bed all day, pull the covers up over your head, and keep on sleeping? Did you want to miss breakfast and lunch and supper and hope everyone would go away?

It is easy to feel that way when things are going badly. People feel blue and want to give up. They want their problems to go away, and they want to stop hurting.

If your parent drinks too much, you have problems. It isn't your imagination. Life is difficult. But staying in bed won't help. Sitting under a tree and tossing stones won't help. Overeating won't help. Breaking windows never helps. Stepping on ants in the driveway doesn't do much either.

One way to feel better about yourself is to look around for someone who needs you. Try to take your eyes off yourself and find another person you can cheer up. There are plenty of people around whom you can help if you will look for them. Who needs help with his or her school work? Who can't get out and needs a visitor? Who needs yard work done? Who would enjoy getting a letter from you? Who could you run an errand for? Who needs to be invited out to play ball?

We all feel sorry for ourselves once in a while because we all have it hard in some way at some time. But if we spend too much time thinking about our problems, we only make things worse. The Bible helps us by reminding us to look out for others. When we make someone else's life easier, we make our lives easier, too. "Each of you should look not only to your own interests, but also to the interests of others" (Philippians 2:4).

◆ ◆ ◆ ◆ ◆

The Sober Parent

If one of your parents *doesn't* have a drinking problem, thank God. Some families have two parents who drink too much, and life is much worse for them.

The wife or husband of someone who has a drinking problem has a tough life. Like a one-armed juggler, he or she sometimes has trouble keeping all the balls in the air at the same time.

These are a few of the problems a sober parent faces:

He or she spends a lot of time trying to cover up for the spouse. Often the sober parent lies, makes excuses, and keeps people away so no one will discover what is going on.

He or she may have trouble admitting that there is a problem.

He or she probably faces financial difficulties. Drinking is usually an expensive drain on the family.

The drinking problem may become the center of the sober parent's life. Most decisions he or she makes are controlled by the alcoholic spouse.

Often the sober parent has great mood
swings—happy one moment, angry the
next. His or her emotions are run by
the spouse's drinking.

Your sober parent isn't all that he or she
would like to be. Without the pressure of an
alcohol problem in the family, your parent might
be much more loving, peaceful, playful, patient,
and available. Be grateful for all the good he or
she does.

Sober parents live under a great deal of pain.
Their marriages aren't going well, and they are
terribly disappointed. Children cannot change
their parents' situation but they can try hard to
be understanding.

We can become more understanding by
learning about alcoholism. Knowledge leads to
understanding. We can also look to God for support. Our belief in God can help us be accepting
of others in spite of their weaknesses.

It's All Right to Love
Your Parent

Should a child love a parent who does harm to others? Should he or she love a parent

who can't be trusted,

who says mean things,

who forgets promises?

Some days it is hard to love a person who behaves like that. We get angry at the person, and at times we might even hate someone

who spends too much,

who stinks from alcohol,

who yells and complains.

Even if a parent does all of this, it is all right to love the parent. You don't *have* to—it is a decision for you to make. But it is okay if you choose to love your parent who drinks too much. If you do, you might want to show your love by

speaking to your parent,

giving him or her a hug, or maybe

helping your parent do something.

The best time to show love or to say how much you love your drinking parent is when he or she is sober. That is when your parent understands love the best.

A child doesn't show love by helping a parent drink. It would be better if you did not

help your parent get alcohol,

lie or make excuses for him or her, or

say that it is all right to drink.

Some children try to stay away from their parents all the time. The alcohol problem makes them feel terrible, and they try to avoid their parents. Others try to be near their parents when they are sober but keep their distance when the parents are drinking. In any case, the best time to show love is when the person knows what is going on.

"And now these three remain: faith, hope and love. But the greatest of these is love"

(1 Corinthians 13:13).

Feeling Embarrassed

The check-out line at the local discount store was crowded. Megan had to pick up a new hair blower, and her friend Katie was along for company.

Finally Megan reached the cashier, and the amount appeared on the register: $18.07. Hurriedly Megan searched through her pockets—first her coat pockets and then her jeans. In a few seconds Katie could see the problem coming.

"I can't believe it," Megan exclaimed. "I must have left my money at home." Katie stood silently, but she could feel her face turn red. She was embarrassed because of Megan's problem.

We all do that some time. Another person makes a mistake or says something really dumb and we blush even though it isn't exactly our problem. We know we didn't do it, but we feel ashamed anyway.

If the person who made a mistake is our relative, we feel even more embarrassed. When our father tells jokes that aren't funny, we blush. If our mother puts a dent in the car, we feel bad that she looks clumsy. Sometimes we feel ashamed because of the behavior of a relative.

When parents drink too much we feel embarrassed. We don't want our friends to see them drunk, and we think our parents make us look bad.

There are two main reasons why we feel embarrassed and ashamed. First, we don't want our friends to think our parents are terrible people. Second, we feel guilty or responsible for our parents.

How can you overcome your embarrassment? The first reason can be helped by saying to your friend, "My mother [or father] has a problem with alcohol." This statement is straightforward and honest. Your friend should not have to guess what is going on. You explained the situation so that everyone will know what is going on.

The second reason can be handled by saying to yourself, "I am not responsible for my parent's drinking problem." We often blush because we feel shame. Our parents' behavior is not *our* behavior. If we get confused and think we are partly to blame, we will feel ashamed.

Some of the embarrassment will still hang around because it is tough to live with a drinking parent. But we can feel less shame if we keep reminding ourselves of these two facts.

Don't punish yourself for someone else's problems. God wants you to know you are innocent and not guilty of your parents' behavior.

"Declare the innocent not guilty" (1 Kings 8:32c).

Jesus Is a Friend

Traci lived next door to Kellie. Kellie was more than a neighbor. She was also a person with whom Traci could play, share school work, and go shopping at the mall. Traci liked Kellie because she was a good listener and someone who shared important things like tapes and games and hot cinnamon rolls.

Kellie was many things to Traci because she was a good friend. Their special relationship was something they enjoyed at home, at school, and even at the local fast-food restaurant.

Each of us can have a special friend in Jesus Christ. Naturally he is more than that. Jesus is many things to us. He is the Son of God, Savior, and Counselor. But he is much more than simply a far-off, powerful person.

As a friend, Jesus is someone

we can talk to,

we can trust in,

we can ask to help calm us down.

As a friend, Jesus is someone

who is always close,

who understands,

who accepts us as we are,

who forgives us when we mess up,

who hates to see us hurt,

who cares.

As a friend, Jesus is someone

who loves us all the time,

who helps us love others,

who helps keep us from going bonkers.

Jesus isn't simply a picture on a wall or a statue in a building. Jesus is more than a figure on a cross. He is more than an interesting person who lived a long time ago.

When we put our faith in Jesus Christ, when we believe in him, he becomes a personal loving friend. Ask Christ to come into your life and be your friend—for today and forever.

"Greater love has no one than this, that he lay down his life for his friends" (John 15:13).

◆ ◆ ◆ ◆ ◆

Is Drunk Better?

This question isn't as silly as it sounds. A few children have lived with an alcoholic parent for so long that they like the parent drunk more than they like him or her sober. Many children probably do not feel this way, but some do.

After living with an alcoholic parent for years, a child tries hard to learn how to get along. The child has to find some way to make life easier.

Some children have learned that when a parent is drunk there are some things they can count on. For instance:

The house may become quieter if the parent gets drunk and passes out.

Children may find it easier to get spending money from a drinking parent.

Children may be able to go out for the evening after their parent starts drinking and becomes quiet.

A drinking parent may no longer insist that the child help with the dishes.

After a few drinks a parent may stop nagging a child about cleaning up his or her room.

After drinking a parent might be more willing to order pizza.

It is hard to live with a parent who drinks too much. That is why some children learn how to make the best of a bad situation. That is easy to understand. If we can't have a sober parent, we have to find a way to live with one who abuses alcohol.

But don't be fooled. Everyone's life would become better if the parent would stop drinking. A clear-thinking, caring, loving, reasonable parent is *always* better.

If your parent gets control over his or her alcohol problem, you will be a much happier person.

However, many children of alcoholic parents grow up to be happy adults. Expect a full, enjoyable life and it probably will be yours.

Continue to learn about alcohol and its effects. Be close to Jesus Christ and his loving process. Become the kind of person you want to be. Many of the people we see getting the most out of life also had alcoholic parents.

◆ ◆ ◆ ◆ ◆

When You Can't Trust Them

At one o'clock sharp, Bridgette sat on a stone bench in front of the Sears store. The huge mall bustled with people hurrying to complete their holiday shopping. Bridgette played with the straw in her soft drink as she waited for her mother. They were going to shop for sweaters for Christmas. Impatiently she checked her watch to discover that ten minutes had passed. Bridgette grew nervous. Her mother was often tardy.

Bridgette tried to stay light-hearted. She hoped that counting people would get her mind off it. Twenty minutes passed. Bridgette's heart sank. This had happened many times before. Her mother had promised to meet her and failed to show.

At 1:45 Bridgette stood up and began walking toward the exit. Her shoulders dropped. Her legs felt heavy. She was almost sure of what had happened. Her mother had probably begun drinking at noon and had forgotten all about her promise.

If a parent has a habit of drinking too much, the children can't trust the parent's promises. They may wish they could trust their parent, but they can't. Their parent has trouble remembering where, when, and who to meet. The parent tells the children she will buy them paper for school but then forgets to pick it up. Or the parent says that it is all right for the child to go to a friend's house, but when the time comes he says no.

If you can't trust your parent, what can you do about it? There are several things you can try. It is important to keep as good an attitude as possible.

1. *Admit it.* You can't trust your parent. Keep trying, but don't pretend that your parent is dependable when he or she isn't. As long as he or she drinks too much, your parent will not be dependable.

2. *Don't blame yourself.* It isn't your imagination; your drinking parent does break promises.

3. *Hang loose.* Try to leave room for your parent's mistakes. Life is difficult to predict, and yours will be a bit more unpredictable.

4. *Trust others.* Not everyone is undependable. Find friends, teachers, coaches, and pastors whom you can trust. The temptation is to trust no one, and that makes life too hard. Let yourself trust God, even if it is a little bit at a time.

5. *Don't become like your parent.* If your parent breaks promises or lies or cheats, you don't have to become like him or her. Be yourself. You know it is right to keep your promises. Don't let your home situation make you someone you don't want to be.

"Do not let your hearts be troubled. Trust in God; trust also in me [Jesus Christ]" (John 14:1).

A Lump in Your Throat

When you have a parent who drinks too much, your feelings are often hurt. You feel disappointed, angry, sad, frustrated.

You wish it would go away, but the drinking stays and so does the pain. You feel confused, hateful, afraid, lonely.

You try to be brave and tough and shake it off like a duck shakes water off its back, but it doesn't shake off easily. You feel tired, let down, cheated, desperate.

Sometimes those feelings hurt too much. A lump begins to form in your throat, and your eyes become moist. You swallow hard or blink to try and fight back the tears.

Your feelings are so strong that you are about to cry. There isn't anything wrong with crying. Let it go and let it flow. Both girls and boys need to cry. Both women and men need to cry. It doesn't help to cry all the time, but sometimes you need to let it out. A good, honest cry may be the perfect thing to do.

Don't be surprised if God cries when you cry. God feels sad about the pain you feel.

"Jesus wept" (John 11:35).

Parent Love

When your parents have been drinking, do you ever say to yourself, "How can they love me and keep doing that?" Many children ask that question. It is a natural question for a child to ask, especially if the parents do things that hurt the child.

It would be easy to say, "Yes, your parents love you." Your parents probably do love you very much. But you aren't looking for another person to tell you that. You want your parents to let you know they love you.

There are two ways that parents can show love. First, they say the words "I love you" or words that mean the same, like "I enjoy having you around" or "You are great to be with." Words are important. We want to hear that a parent loves us.

Second, parents do things for the child they love. They act in a loving way. Loving parents spend time with you, get food for you, supply clothes for you, help when you have problems, talk to you, and listen. Loving parents want to help.

When parents drink too much, their ability to talk and act in a loving way gets messed up. Too often they say mean things instead of kind things, and they do painful things rather than caring things. They frequently hurt the people they love. That sounds goofy, and it is goofy, but too much alcohol makes people goofy.

If a person hurts the people he or she loves, how will those people figure out that they are loved? That's hard, and sometimes they can't figure it out. Your parent may love you with all of his or her heart but can't show you that love because the alcohol stops your parent from showing love in the right way.

Does your parent love you? Most likely. But the alcohol has messed up his or her love system. When your parent is able to get free from the alcohol, he or she may be able to show real love.

◆ ◆ ◆ ◆ ◆

Handle Today

When Cody was three years old, he couldn't read the newspaper. He was bright and liked books, but he definitely couldn't read the newspaper. At the age of nine Cody could read very well, and he felt good about what he could do.

One day Cody decided that he wished he had been able to read when he was three. Now Cody wanted to turn back the calendar and learn to read at the age of three.

Cody can't do that. He can't change yesterday. The best thing he can do is enjoy reading today and leave the past alone.

There are things in our past that we wish we could change, but we can't. Smart people make the most of today, because worrying about yesterday doesn't help.

Cody liked to use his imagination. Often he would wonder about what might happen tomorrow. Suppose, he asked himself, something happened to his mind and he forgot how to read. Cody pictured himself waking up one morning, looking at a book cover, and not being able to read the title. He would never be able to read again! Thinking about it scared Cody almost out of his shoes.

Quickly Cody collected big stacks of books, magazines, newspapers, and brochures. He wasn't going to play ball today. He decided to eat in his bedroom. No television, no video games, no talking; Cody would spend all day reading everything he could, because, as he imagined, he might forget how to read tomorrow and never be able to read again.

Cody was going to lose all the good things about today because he was totally worried over what might happen tomorrow. Smart people make the most of today, because worrying about tomorrow doesn't help.

Jesus teaches us to handle one day at a time. Worrying about yesterday and tomorrow only messes up today.

"Therefore do not worry about tomorrow, for tomorrow will worry about itself. Each day has enough trouble of its own" (Matthew 6:34).

◆ ◆ ◆ ◆ ◆

A Sore Thumb

Did you ever hit yourself on the thumb with a hammer? You probably yelled, ran cold water over your thumb, and maybe even sucked it for a bit. Two-year-olds, twelve-year-olds, and twenty-year-olds all seem to react the same way to a banged thumb.

If you broke the skin or split the nail, you wrapped the wound in a bandage. The thumb probably thumped with pain for part of the day, and you treated it carefully. Whenever you bumped your thumb against a chair or forgot and grabbed a doorknob, you yelped again in pain.

There are four other fingers on your hand, but while your thumb throbbed, you didn't pay much attention to the other members. You took them for granted. It was the hurting member that was on your mind most of the time.

When a member of the family has a serious drinking problem, that person is the hurting thumb. The majority of the family's time and energy is used worrying about and trying to help that member. It isn't fair to ignore the rest of the family. Everyone has needs. Everyone has problems. Everyone has joys, accomplishments, and happy moments. Those people and those times need attention, too.

Understandably, the hurting person who drinks too much needs extra attention. If the person doesn't get it, he or she often demands it. But the entire family has to work to keep everything in close balance. Never ignore the rest of the family and put everyone's interest on the sore thumb. Spend time with brothers, sisters, and the dog. Play ball with the nondrinking parent. Get out a board game and enjoy being a family as much as you can.

The sore thumb is not the whole hand. Go to a school program, go to a movie, get into snowball fights with the neighbor kids. Every member of the family counts.

◆ ◆ ◆ ◆ ◆

Many Parents Get Better

A drinking problem wears everyone out. Arguments, complaining, lack of money, name calling, undependability, loss of love, and poor health are only some of the seemingly endless agonies and pain. You and other members of your family may wish and pray that the drinking would stop and you could be happy together.

Don't give up hope. No one can promise that things will get better. Some parents are slaves to alcohol all their lives. But there is also a large number of parents who recover and lead normal lives again. Your dreams can come true.

Usually a parent must find help if he or she is to get better. Drinking problems are often too difficult to overcome alone. Many people say they can quit drinking whenever they want, but that is almost never true. A counselor, an organization like Alcoholics Anonymous, or a clinic is almost always needed if the problem is to be handled successfully. The parent must realize the consequences of his or her drinking.

There are *many* people who used to get drunk often, and today they no longer drink. They now enjoy their children and have a happy family.

Dream of the day when you might live with a sober parent again. Don't count on the dream, don't live on the dream, but pray to keep the hope alive.

"Love . . . always hopes" (1 Corinthians 13:6-7).

◆ ◆ ◆ ◆ ◆

What Is a Recovering Alcoholic?

Jeremy was a young man of average size—not too thin and not too heavy. All of his friends called him Jeremy because that was his name. But occasionally someone would call him "Chubs." To look at him the nickname seemed strange.

The people who called him "Chubs" were the ones who knew Jeremy as a teenager. In high school he was overweight by twenty pounds, and his friends kidded him about it. While in college Jeremy lost weight. He watched what he ate and exercised because he wanted to avoid gaining too much weight again.

A recovering alcoholic is someone who used to have problems created by drinking. Most recovering alcoholics have stopped drinking altogether and now lead sober lives. However, they know that alcohol could become a problem again. "Recovering" means he or she must be careful all of his or her life. The recovering alcoholic dares not look at alcohol as a simple beverage that he or she can drink without worrying about it. People who work with alcoholics say they might never be able to safely use alcohol again. Usually a recovering alcoholic is someone who has had an alcohol problem but has stopped drinking.

◆ ◆ ◆ ◆ ◆

It Takes Time to Stop

If a car is traveling at sixty-five miles an hour, it cannot stop at a stop sign. The car has picked up too much speed to stop all at once. A moving car has something called "inertia." That means that it will continue to move forward until something slows it down or stops it. The automobile must slow down gradually—fifty-five, forty-five, twenty-five—before it can stop at the sign. An average car can't stop in a split second.

When a person has a serious drinking problem, the body and mind are used to alcohol, sometimes large amounts of alcohol. If the person decides to stop drinking, he or she will have trouble quitting all at once. The drinker may put the bottle or can down and refuse to drink another drop of alcohol, but the adjustment can really be hard. The person's drinking was traveling at full speed, and the change can be tough.

Be patient with a parent who has stopped drinking. His or her mood may get grouchy. Sometimes he or she may feel sick. A parent may have to attend many meetings and counseling sessions. Mom or Dad may have to be away from the house for weeks or even months getting help. Your parent is adjusting to the stop just as a speeding car needs to gradually brake to a halt.

Most of us want to see a cure and see it right now. That is easy to understand. Many children have gone through years of misery because their parents drank too much. Now your parent is seeking help. Don't run out of patience. You can see the goal line. Your parent is not going to be perfect, but what a great change there will be. Expect some days to go better than others. Such a dramatic change is not likely to happen easily. The cells in your parent's brain and heart are trying to get used to not having alcohol. Some of those tiny cells have been damaged by getting too much alcohol for years. He or she probably isn't used to eating right or sleeping right or getting good exercise. The body is coming back to full life again.

If your parent is finding help, thank God for the progress. The change won't be easy, but it will certainly be worth it.

◆ ◆ ◆ ◆ ◆

Will You Become An Alcoholic?

You may have heard it at school. Or maybe you saw it on television or read it in the newspaper. Some people believe that if parents drink too much their children will grow up to drink too much also. Like father, like son. Like mother, like daughter.

But is it true? Do children grow up to drink alcohol the same way their parents drink it?

Not many of us grow up to be exactly like our parents. A son may not like to work on cars even if his father enjoyed tinkering with them. A mother may love to cook, yet her daughter can't stand to be in the kitchen.

We are individuals. We make choices. Your mother may love to eat banana cream pie, but to you it tastes like an old sock.

Most of the time we are like our parents in some ways but very different in other ways. Maybe both you and your parents like movies, but they prefer old ones and you like new ones. You're similar, but you aren't exactly alike.

You know there is an alcohol problem in your family—a parent who drinks too much. Maybe there are other members of your family such as an uncle or an aunt or a grandparent who also drink too much.

When you see alcohol as a problem in your family, a red flag should go up in your mind. You have reason to look very closely at your use of alcohol and your attitude toward it.

What if you pick up your parent's habit?

What if you have his or her exact body chemistry?

What if you choose to deal with problems the same way your parent deals with them?

What if you think you need alcohol to feel relaxed?

What if you enjoy drinking alone?

What if you need alcohol to be accepted by your friends?

All of us have reason to be concerned about alcohol. But if we have relatives who drink too much, we have *extra* reason to be concerned.

That doesn't mean we will become alcoholics, but it does mean we would be fools to ignore how much damage alcohol can do to people.

When we make decisions about alcohol, we can turn to God for assistance. God will stand by and help us make the right choices if we ask God to. We don't have to resist alcohol entirely by ourselves.

"No temptation has seized you except what is common to man. And God is faithful; he will not let you be tempted beyond what you can bear. But when you are tempted, he will also provide a way out so that you can stand up under it" (1 Corinthians 10:13).

◆ ◆ ◆ ◆ ◆

The Green Shoes

When she saw them in the store window, Polly loved the idea right away. Her mother wasn't so sure, but finally she gave in. Polly got a brand-new pair of bright green shoes.

Since they were everyday shoes, Polly began wearing them to school. She loved the attention. Her friends talked about them. They teased and acted shocked. One friend said she wished she had a pair just like them. A couple of Polly's teachers mentioned the shoes. Miss Harmon actually blushed when she saw them.

The first week was fun; the shoes caused a lot of attention and made Polly the talk of the school. The second week things calmed down because people had become used to Polly's shoes. By the third week Polly had become "the girl with the green shoes." Students started saying things like, "Oh, you mean the girl with the green shoes?" or "Let's give that to the girl with the green shoes." One day a teacher called on Polly in class by saying, "Okay, you with the green shoes."

Polly didn't like what she had become. She was no longer just Polly. Instead of being looked at as a person, her shoes seemed more important than she was.

Each of us is, first of all and primarily, a person. You aren't merely the son of the mechanic or the daughter of the lawyer. Neither are you first of all the child of an alcoholic. The most important thing about anyone is that he or she is a person.

The danger is that you may talk so much about your parent's drinking problem that it seems to become the only thing in your life. While the problem is big, it is not all there is about you. You are still a student, friend, ball player, painter, dreamer, video game player, camper, singer, magician, and joke teller. The problem your parent has with alcohol is only part of your life. You don't want to become just "the child of an alcoholic," because you are far more than that.

When God looks at you does God see only the child of an alcoholic? No. God knows that you are, but God also knows that you are far more. Each of us is a person. First we are Megan or Derrick or Benjamin or Katie. Having alcoholic parents is only one aspect of our lives.

God also sees you as his child. By faith in Jesus Christ as your Savior you become part of God's family. You are not just a child with a problem. Each of us is a full, interesting person whom God loves very much.

"How great is the love the Father has lavished on us, that we should be called the children of God! And that is what we are" (1 John 3:1).

Grow Up to Be a Firefighter

What do some children of alcoholics become when they grow up?

Some are singers.

Some are fishers.

Some are bankers.

Some are turkey-pluckers.

89

If you meet children of alcoholics on the street, they look like everyone else. You can't pick them out at a party.

Some are race car drivers.

Some are ministers.

Some are dancers.

Some are candy-twisters.

Children of alcoholics don't have three ears or ride pogosticks to work. You can sit beside one on the city bus and never know that his or her parents drink too much.

Some are farmers.

Some are doctors.

Some are engineers.

Some are human cannonballs.

If you go to a concert and look up and down the rows of people, you can't guess who the children of alcoholics are. They don't all wear red hats or bow ties that light up.

Some are accountants.

Some are plumbers.

Some are writers.

Some are scuba divers.

The whole world is open, and children of alcoholics can choose their own careers. Often they are extremely successful in their jobs. Often they study hard, work hard, and become bosses.

Some are bakers.

Some are clerks.

Some are factory workers.

Some are clowns.

Grown children of alcoholics may have had a rough childhood, and they may have some unpleasant memories. They may still feel sad and angry now and then. But their past doesn't stop them from reaching out and becoming what they want to be.

Some are reporters.

Some are cooks.

Some are actors.

Some are bull riders.

The children of alcoholics grow up to become just like other people.

It Isn't Fair

No, it isn't fair.
Sometimes life is unfair,
but God stays close
when things go well
and when the going
gets tough.

"Cast all your anxiety on him because he cares for you" (1 Peter 5:7).